For the Star that May Have Died

For the Star that May Have Died

Poetry and Prose by Nicole Andonov

The New York Quarterly Foundation, Inc.
New York, New York

NYQ Books™ is an imprint of The New York Quarterly Foundation, Inc.

The New York Quarterly Foundation, Inc.
P. O. Box 2015
Old Chelsea Station
New York, NY 10113

www.nyqbooks.org

First Edition

Set in New Baskerville

Layout and Design by Raymond P. Hammond
Cover Art by Monique Leite

Library of Congress Control Number: 2012949935

ISBN: 978-1-935520-73-3

For the Star that May Have Died

Acknowledgments

My thanks to the editors of journals and anthologies who previously published some of the poems included here:

Barrow Street: "Cafard," "Hyperbole"
Poetry in Performance: "A Viewer like You," "The Purling River,"
   "Babylon Next," "The Year of Magical Thinking"
6x6 #8 (Ugly Duckling Presse): "Late," "The Gesture," "Walking #32"
We Remember 9 /11: "The Gesture"
Goodbye Blue Monday: "Ah the Glitter!"
92nd Street Y, 60+ Anthologies: "Aubergines," "Census 2010"
   "Eyjafjallajökul," "For the Star that may have died," "In Answer to
   your Questions," "Preludes," "Southold," "Summer 2010,"
   "Moon," "What Remains"
The Cento–a collection of Collage Poems: "Morning with Pessoa"

My grateful appreciation goes to Raymond Hammond for his invitation to submit to NYQ Books, and all the work he and The New York Quarterly Foundation, Inc. provided to bring these pages to life.

My thanks also go to Elaine Equi, Hermine Meinard, Barry Wallenstein, Martine Bellen, Dennis Nurkse, Jean Valentine, Sheila Kholer, Allen Davis 3rd, Jason Shinder and the New School poets, Margaret Ryan, Lorna Knowles Blake, Frances Richey, Emily Claman and the 92nd Street Y, 60 + poets who have helped these poems grow.

A very special hug to Frances Richey, Helen Tzagoloff, and Manny Leite for their valuable suggestions in shaping this book.

Warm kisses to the members of my family who read me patiently, lexicon in hand, and asked me to be more conversational, less cryptic. I listened.

To you, my readers: Thank you for buying this book, and for enjoying it.

n.a.

for my children

with love

Contents

I

II

III

IV

V

VI

For the Star that May Have Died

I

For the Star that May Have Died

after Edward Hirsch

Today I want to say something wonderful
for the star that may have recently died
in our galaxy; I want to say something wonderful
for the supernova drumming the Alaskan snow,
melting glaciers, freezing the tropics.

Not that I particularly love mud-lava-fire-
smoke-tsunami-drought and seism,
but, wouldn't it be awesome
if New Orleans rose above sea level, and Tibet
became more hospitable? Wouldn't it be brilliant
to have tropical winters infusing temperate energy
and curbing the urge to create so many
who cannot feed themselves?

We drink our cup of tea
expecting the skies to safeguard our ways,
disperse our "truths," and fill our nights with stars.
That's why I want to say something astonishing
like: The Earth is building a new Earth.

Let it blanket our capitol with a broad bank of snow;
let it hem in the exuberant will to do, or to have done.
Let it warm the polar cap. I'd love to find myself
in the fluting of a luminous aurora
open-armed, head tilted toward heaven, feet deep
in a young field of wheat, whirling…

Babylon Next

Black umbrellas pivot in a blue storm like tops
rushing to the gutter.
Your legs are bent, sinking into your toes.
Your head lights up.

The target is the earth;
the aim, the moon.

A scissors of a man, rolling two balls on his biceps,
advances toward you *en pointes.*
He comes forward and passes.
His light cuts in.

It's been raining for months
and everything has turned green,

elsewhere.
Here, the gray lake has reached the tracks.
Black birds, relentlessly, oil their feathers.
Where have the swans gone?

It's a crisis
that fills basements with grime.

The week is ending.
Halfway around the earth, the week is starting—
a phenomenon that has the power to move
the entire world on a spin.

On the platform a man offers a flowered umbrella
to every woman who steps into the rain.

Green Peppercorn

I lost an earring
on the subway track
and suddenly felt naked.
Such a small thing;
such a huge gap!
First thing out on the street
got myself a brand new pair.

I lie. All poets do, don't they?
I speak of earrings, a small item
that could be a brooch, a clip, a hair,
the heel on my pump, or yours,
a late husband, a late wife or lover.
It could be the loss of a virginal state,
her loose bladder, his dysentery,
the jeering of a fleeting word,
a pitch missing in your tonality
or the loss of hope on the threshold of death
—a small item.

Dying for Air

The roof leaks
smothering tar
leaks limestone tar
leaks lime stones.
I scoop the tar barehanded.
The blocks crumble.

*

Dangling on a plumb line
I hold Ariadne's clew
strung to a quill
juggling flaxed gossamers
swirling on gravity.
Polarized skulls
twirl endlessly.

*

I rise.
My eyes search
beyond charred lashes
unattending other selves.
A hand clasps my temples.
Frozen reflex.

*

Corpses glide
entwine necklaces tight
around my neck.
My head bursts
scatters beads unstrung.
I skid
on a stream of onyx.
I run arms sprung.

Aubade with No Goodbyes (1944)

In silence, not to awaken
his mother, father, and older sister,
Andon dressed hastily,

retrieved from under his pillow
a small woolen bag
he had packed the previous night.

In it: photos, birth certificate,
a lock of his girlfriend's hair,
and eight gold coins

the tooth fairy had left in his shoes
when he was growing up
in the old house

long before he had gone to war
and the State had taken
his parents' lands and factories,

and they had found themselves
living and sleeping all together
in that one-room dwelling.

Noiselessly, he closed the door
after him, and stepped out
into the semi-darkness—

Along the beaten-earth road
his parents had planted a row
of laurel and flat beds of dahlias.

At the rear of the tiny lot,
they had tilled a vegetable garden,
fenced with grape espaliers

where his mother had sat on her heels,
binding the cabbage leaves.

I've Never Wanted a Bone-colored Bathtub Though They Were Once Fashionable

I've seen bathtubs change from antique white to dusty olive, then to bright maize casting the sun upon sadness. I've seen the wine tub where I drank Baudelaire bloom roses. I've seen mink collars propped up on black cashmere; feathered hats brushing my earlobes come back anew on the pages of *Vogue*. I've felt the swirls of pastel beads on baby-pink sweaters, and minis climb mini-mini above my knees before they swept the floor. I've seen men's lapels shrink, and their chests bulk out. I've hemmed bell-bottoms and tapered slacks, turned cuffs up and let them down. I've rested my pearled gloves on his broad shoulders, and held his shriveled hands when they grew cold. I've watched my children stretch to many wondrous and splendorous things. I've seen the dead immured in stone. I've seen them buried in wood, and glass coffins, or marble urns. It would be altogether fitting, would it not, that my ashes be blown upon the Prospect Park Meadow, where my kids played baseball on former tennis courts, and when now, on Sunday mornings the canine pedigree, and most ordinary run, carefree.

A Place to Rest

I chose this lot because of the dogwood
spreading petals uneven,

a parasol
fluttering the breeze.

It's odd to think *delicate*
for sturdy:

our first kiss
quickening the Palisades,

highway dogwoods
lacing the wind.

I found a hole by its roots,
gypsy moths, long-horned beetles,

ants hauling carcasses, to
or from.

Each time I blocked the opening
the stone I wedged in was nudged out.

"The dogwood is diseased,"
the caretaker said. "It will have to be removed."

Chagrin

Until the psalms were silent
Until the flowers were dry
Until I assumed his work
Until the children graduated
Until my brother moved away
Until my son moved away
Until my daughter moved away
Until silence grew cold
Until my son's classmate died
Until we paid our respects
Until I held the mother's hand
Until I said: "So young!"
Until she said, "Yes, so young."

On the Avenue

In the dream, I was walking with my husband, looking for him. Carefully we both, on account of love, thought perhaps we might find the man we lost. At the corner bus stop, a child stood in a daze. He was very thin, almost bony, and his arms, his legs shrinking so small, so small. I picked him up, on love's account and gave him to the nurse at the "drugstore pharmacy." She was concerned—which pleased me. She didn't want him though, gave him back to me, stiff as a board, wrapped in a blanket. "It's yours," she said. I held him close, so close, his hands cuddled around my breast, on love's account. "Bus's coming," someone called. Still holding on to the baby, I rushed towards the door. "The buses never come on time," the baby said.

Tuscan Light

There are dark rectangular holes on the second floor, right below the striped roof across the vineyard. (The roof must've suffered over the years, and whole rows of tiles had to be replaced with new.) A swarm of butterflies alights the front entrance by the arched portico. Cypresses and *parasol* pines stretch their shadows on the chartreuse grass. (Why call them "umbrella" pines when there's no trace of rain, and the sun fills every crevice, every yellow cup of desire with gladness as calm as the rows of vines tilled from the stoned earth?)

I wish I could think of you as a person, but you are only a thought sniffing with me the daisies lining the road, picking buttercups and wild roses along the abandoned path; only a shadow preceding me in this vast panorama where little nothings repeat themselves as redundant echoes, where I am the same as always, and you are the same, a bright spot among the brambles.

The light has taken you away, only a minute at a time, very sporadically, but you are still here preceding, following, amplified like a cliché that repeats, repeats on everyone's lips, though you are mine, mine alone.

The Eyes We Close

Eyes shining without mystery

to open
so many eyes
in the body

They sleep in the depth of tombs
and the eyes fill up with shadows

held together
by no more
than a thought

just as you
are no more
than a thought

to open like
so many eyes
on the other side of the tombs.

II

Hyperbole

She rides each curve
keeping a constant distance
from blunder and discomfort.

Her range of fireworks
is proportionate to the enthusiasm
that wills it.

Zest is function occasion essence extract
an appetite for the condiment
a rhythm to circumvent.

What would she say to this?
Yves's husband was squashed between two cars.
Every day a new cab every day a new driver
Every day a bomb
somewhere.
A rash spreading like strawberries on your forehead
your chest your legs.

The facts are simple:
Eat artichokes one leaf at a time
Let the cherry trees bloom on the riverside
Let feet trample on the sand of Jones Beach.
Take a ride in the park.
The lake is calm. People row their boats.

She'll bring you the sun on fire with a glorious array of marigolds.

In Answer to Your Questions

I am cherry jubilee, flambé in kirsch—
no, I'm not. I am blue. (I don't know why intense
or still blue is the exclusive of little boys, and depression.)
I am the blue of Capri, of Marseille, the blue
of Torvill and Dean—the blue veil
of Torvill and Dean as they ice-danced to a perfect 10;
I'm the royal blue of the Oldsmobile I filled with tiles,
saddles, wallpapers. I gave the car away
when it wanted to give me up.

I used to love the violin and the harp.
My ears can't accommodate strings any longer.
This morning WQXR was see-sawing Bach on my eardrums
and on a copy of a *Young Woman Sewing in the Garden*
my husband had offered me
when he wanted his shirt collars turned over.
(Who ever thought of reversing collars?)

I still love the piano. In my childhood
we had a Steinway where I wanted to compose,
not practice. As the piano stayed idle for a year,
and mother couldn't make ends meet, she decided to sell it.
Before the movers could take it away, I climbed onto the truck,
and ting-ting-tingged and tap-tap-tapped, and cliiiingged,
flaunting all the octaves I remembered,
playing to the piano my fondest cacophony.

If I were a tree, I'd be a frail, knotty, serviceable,
ordinary birch, peeling the seasons, vibrating the breeze.
Sorry, I can't see myself as an animal (we've traveled such perils
becoming humans); never wanted to be a number
among numbers—not a 3, not a 7, not 3.1416, not infinity.
Hey Number 5! Number 54! I couldn't answer to that.

I could be a number of individuals, one at a time—
Jane Austen, Marie Curie, Flaubert…
I could even be numerous. I was happy being two people
for a while, then three, then four, then three again,
and now seven and three-quarters
with a round belly and little feet pat-a-patting.
It's fascinating the way we eclipse into a new smile,
in a curtain of volition gone impervious.

The last time I saw Paris,
there was a McDonald's and bums *sur Les Champs-Élysées.*
Here, the homeless camped on the steps of St. Thomas—
the Episcopalian church on 1 W. 53rd Street;
Job Lot had opened on 39th, Altman's had closed,
and Fifth Avenue had moved to Madison.

I'm afraid of words I can't take back
after I've uttered them, like the proverbial feathers
blown on the crest of a gusty hill;
I'm afraid of wrong decisions—choosing a too-light grout
that frames the tiles apart; or renting part of my house
to a scourge I can't dislodge.

My dreams have faded in reed-pipes,
to steady my blood surge low.
No longer an idealist by empathy, nor a realist
by principle, I swing like a birch with each passing wind—
no—against each passing wind, it seems.

Ruminations

In my twenties, doing away with myself seemed a magical escape from love, deception, embarrassment—and most of all, from an absurd world. I imagined all sorts of ways of dying without it being labeled suicide. Suicide was men jumping head first from the Empire State Building when their fortunes vanished; salmon rushing up a treacherous stream to satisfy instinct; or the legendary pelican, returning empty-pouched from a long fishing trip, opening his guts to feed his young. Dying was romantic—a counterpart to an existential era. It was Greta Garbo's last breath, and camellias, camellias floating on a pond…

Now that I'm eighty, death is abstract; my house a number—its market price. (Will my children be forced to sell, to pay for my demise?) Far are the many birthdays we celebrated within its framed wainscots and abundant windows facing the park. I don't think of Michael and Ivanka, and their friends, Patrick and Sarah and Irene, playing in the sun, in the rain, in the snow, in "my park" across the avenue. I don't hear my children's tricycle making rounds from the living room to the playroom. I don't hear echoes of the *Child's Garden of Verses* up in the air, "up in the air so blue," nor the munchkins' refrain on the yellow brick road. I don't see myself with trembling hands, injecting insulin in Andon's thighs. Now, that death has turned my life into numbers, I think of putting my papers in order. And I postpone…

Walking with My Younger Sister

It's Sunday, after lunch. The sun shines
on the last golden leaves falling on the park side.
We walk slowly from 13th Street to Grand Army Plaza
stopping at every bench, or two.

We rest on the benches, looking at limestone villas,
brick buildings freshly pointed.
Even the stoop that's been sinking for three decades
is propped up. My sister walks with a cane
willing her feet up and down, one step
then another, and another. Gone the days
when she hauled on high heels an oversized portfolio
holding her breath down the subway steps.

My sister always muted her pains, kept them to herself.
Now, on the park side, she retrains, and hopes.

Table d'Hôte

I

Au
ber
gines

Whenever
I see an eggplant,
its coarse lobed leaves
hiding its purple fruits,
I think of Margaret Mead's
aborigines hanging weights on
their breasts to elongate them as
a status symbol, and flipping them
over their shoulders like long scarves
when cooking or carrying an infant.
In the past, whenever I chose eggplants
at a farmer's market or my neighborhood
store, I thought of Malcom Bosse and the
first time I read boobs referring to women's
breasts. I haven't cooked eggplants since my
husband died. When Andon was alive, I used
to slice the vegetable or fruit (whichever you
want to call it) in halves, disgorge its bitter taste,
empty its inside, cube it, stir-fry it with ground
meat, cooked rice, green peppers, and the yoke
of an egg, stuff & sprinkle it with breadcrumbs.
Andon also loved moussaka and ratatouille,
even ate *aubergines gratinées au parmesan,*
the way I preferred them, although he
thought I had ruined their flavor.
Eggplant was his favorite
vegetable.

II

En Famille

aah!

Then came the bones:
there here before
a chamber full
sad faces limp bodies.
That afternoon in the cemetery,
he presented her to his father.
Wiped the stone clean;
held her close stroked her back.
The dogwoods were in bloom.

Belgian pastry:
Lemon-apple crust
Espresso-nut-crown
Tulips, tulips turning up.

He lays them flat, belly up, on the kitchen counter—
pale, sallow fish from the bottom of the sea.
He slices off the flesh from the bones
the flesh from the skin. I roll them up, poach them
in the broth she's prepared: heads, bones, skin,
shallot, a fresh *bouquet garni*, and a flavor of Riesling.
I arrange them like a flower in a round flat dish,
pour over a béchamel, bake them lightly,
a pat of butter on each.
At the center of the sole petals,
un fond d'artichaut.

III

Delphian Green

I bit on a green olive right off a tree
by Apollo's temple
overlooking the Corinthian gulf.

No wonder that to quell its bitterness
the olive demands so much preparation:
soak, pre-wash, wash, after-wash,
re-soak, process, and salt.

The first time I ate one out of a jar,
I wondered why my parents loved them.
It's like caviar, anchovy, or foie gras,
you've got to acquire the taste.

My niece said her favorite food
is truffle soufflé she had for lunch
at her grandmother's. She could eat it
every day and never tire, she added.

I said she'd have to pick a rich husband.
Her mother countered: "No,
she'd have to choose a prosperous career."

Like caviar and olives,
self-reliance is an acquired taste.

IV

Brioches

The French has less head and more belly—in this recipe—twice the amount of butter (no fear), seven eggs beaten whole two by two, one on top. American: four eggs—one white whipped separately with sugar to brown. Although both versions scald milk, beat and knead dough, the French calls for slapping, banging, punching—a real workout. The American is partly democratic, served commonly in coffee shops and stands at train stations, but the French—*Quelle brioche!* It is said the mere allusion to feed it to the poor in lieu of bread evolved into a bloody bath with a number of heads sliced off. The American recipe makes sixteen brioches; the French, eighteen—perhaps to avoid any link to Louis XVI or October 16. Oven-baked, both are done in fifteen minutes. It's the preparation that consumes—pinching, fondling, plus three to four warm hours for the dough to rise, overnight or longer to chill.

V

Château Rayme Vigneau

This corked and sealed Château Rayme Vigneau premier grand cru '79 Sauternes has been in my refrigerator door for 3 decades. This was the year when all wines, any wine, grand cru or most ordinary, flattered the palate with a taste of heaven. This was the year when poor Aunt Odette stayed over for an extended visit on her way to Florida where she died recently of diabetic complications.

Aunt Odette loved sweets: crème brûlée, caramel pudding, poire flambée, mousse à l'orange, au chocolat, hand in hand with sweet wines. We had already adopted the eat-and-go-do-something-better attitude. With her, we slipped back to the pleasures of the table. Arched on the kitchen table, her hair in a bun on the back of her neck, she caressed, cuddled, fondled her creations with an amorous desire to please. After preparation and after dinner, she always gathered all leftover dough, crumbs and drops of liqueurs to bake on her last day a bread pudding as she had, trapped in Paris with no supplies, running in and out of air raids.

Once she opened a bottle of Chianti, the fat-belly one, raffia-covered, for an Italian evening of love songs, clams and pasta. "The palate is a better judge than the wallet" she said as she showed us its ticket price of $2.99.

Aunt Odette left. We stopped having desserts with sweet wine. The bottle of sauternes '79 remained in the refrigerator door unnoticed amid juice, quart of milk, and jars of condiments. Today, I'll open it to commemorate her passing. Will it have turned to vinegar like so many sweet memories do after a lifetime of reverence?

VI

Chanterelles

"Ah! Chanterelles," she said, "Chanterelles!
Lisichki in Russian.
Golden crown of summer. Apricotine. I love them."
She thinks I'm Russian, gives me the word, the poem.

Should she serve chanterelles to everyone she meets,
lisichki might mushroom overnight on the pages we read.
The power of dandelions blown.

Were I to say: "*Jack-my-lantern* of the mushroom world,"
would *Clitocybe illudens*, "Angel of death,"
sweep over rhyme and meter?

At the Church of the Miracle
bright red tomatoes mushroom in the snow.
Mushroom: a verb; Chanterelles: a melody.

VII

Cervelle en beignets
for Felicia Equi

I'm tired of snails and frog legs
cervelle au beurre noir,
tired of *testicules* and *gras double*
Rognons sur gazon.
I'm tired of liver *sauce ravigote*
filet chasseur, terrine de lièvre,
cœur de bœuf matelote
under thyme and laurel.
I'm tired of soufflés and *timbales,*
coquilles farcies,
queus en hochepot, raifort saucière,
tripe from Caen, *soupes aux moules,*
crevettes and *langoustes*
and *grenouilles* again!

And When I Come Back, I've Gone

—Pablo Neruda

split halfway across the mountain apices
that undermine the sky

through your dreams:

wild storms
kept tame
numb

lingering on the blue tiles of the rooftop.

Firs recall the distance
from their fields of ivy

lush
aloof

driven like a float of medusae.

Remember:
"Toes are fingers that have forgotten their past."

Green Pleasant and More

The envelopes are stuffed, stamped, addressed,
inviting family and friends to the altar
set on the lawn. (It's September; the lawn's
still green—should we liven it up with rose petals?)

It won't rain that day and the sun will be mild.
(On the 17th of September, Virgo always complies.)
My daughter, radiant, on the arm of my son,
in her elegant satin gown and 5 long-stemmed calla lilies
will enter on a trail of light and multi-colored bubbles.
(Should rose petals be strewn on the aisle?)

Champagne toasts and cocktails will be around the pool,
a gardenia floating in a glass bowl on each table.
(Should rose petals be strewn by the pool?
Should we have candles floating in the water?)

The hors d'oeuvres will be delicious (I wonder
why dinner should follow; it's never as palatable). Ah,
but we'll be seated. The groom will be roasted,
my sister will say three words, my brother three more
before leading my daughter across the dance floor.
She'll gather her train, arc it around her little finger,
and will step to the brilliance of a Viennese waltz.

The band will play Sinatra, Nat King Cole, Elvis, Strauss,
and rounds from Croatia. All will join in—but first,
her unmarried girlfriends will be introduced
to bachelor friends of bride and groom in an informal
foxtrot lesson. (She has so many single friends to root for,
she won't toss her bouquet, nor her garter. She'll pin a corsage
on each girlfriend, a boutonniere on each bachelor,
hoping that more than one will discover an other.)

Not a Cloud in the Blue

Not a cloud in the sky.
Cherry pink and apple-blossom white.

Here they are on the tenth floor,
the mother, no color on her cheeks,
and the little one, trying to suck
and not knowing how
brushing her lips off the nipple.

"Take a picture of mom nursing."
Snapshot of Papap holding the newborn.
Snapshot of Gama taking pictures.
"Do you want to hold her, grandma?"
I'm "grandma," the new grandma
who doesn't yet know how.

Down below in the courtyard
Cherry pink and apple-blossom white.

Here, above the city's rooftops
a serene view of the Hudson
wrapping its arm around us.
Mangoes cut in the shape of flowers.
Apple cider in champagne glasses.
Cheers to mother, father and child.
Cheers to us too.

Not a cloud in the blue.

I shade the glare above her eyes.
The image of my son just a day old,
her lips quite formed,
her little tongue alive against the calm
of the river wrapping itself around us
with cherry pink and apple-blossom white.

Edward Jacques Is Two

He has discovered the word *mine*,
and the secret of possession:
something like "What's mine is mine;
what's yours is mine too
if I want it."

He has discovered
the secret of command:
He fetches the outfit he fancies,
hands it to you with confidence:
"Here Grandma."
You put away the brown corduroy,
slip on the orange waterproof.
Done.

He has discovered
the fine art of the grin,
acknowledging he knows as well as you
he's doing something naughty.
Will you enforce, play his game,
or pay no attention?
His puzzle. And yours.

He has discovered
how to reward your allegiance
with a disarming shrill-jump welcome:
the exclusive grandma special
that conquers you.

Oh, Edward Jacques!

One Little Sparrow

From her stroller, my granddaughter threw a piece of her cracker to a sparrow hopping in the playground. As if by magic, ten more sparrows and two pigeons appeared. Ella threw a bigger piece. A pigeon pecked on it but let the smaller birds feast on. Ella then threw the rest of the cracker. At that very instant, a sparrow swooped down from a tree, snatched the entire piece and flew away. None of the others seemed to mind. I was surprised (and baffled) but Ella clapped, and asked for more crackers. She threw large pieces, and every time, one little sparrow would swoop down from a tree, snatch the whole thing, fly away, and none of the others would fuss. Ella squealed as she does at the puppet show when the big bad wolf blows the house down.

III

Towers (2001)

and then, your son called he was safe; and your daughter had gone to work too early, crossing Canal before; and her friend was so tired, she had shut her alarm off and overslept; and your friend was preparing to join her husband at the plaza when he called to let her know; and her cousin who worked on the 92nd floor had gone that very same day for a job interview; and your next-door neighbor who's been having a bagel and coffee each morning at her desk on the 88th floor had tried for the first time the restaurant on the 70th; and that man was on vacation; and this one had taken a week off to get married; and that one was celebrating his granddaughter's birthday; and these two women had gone on business overseas; and this one never knew what held her back; and the firefighter, who had been climbing upstairs, with axe and hose and all sorts of rescue equipment had to turn back and manage the crowd rushing down; and the paraplegic was carried down to a working elevator eight floors below; the tourists and their children had, since very early on, cancelled their sightseeing tours; and all these people who were supposed to be there— and were not, sparkled like clear crystalline droplets splashing from a deep waterfall basin where pine tree shadows had plunged.

The Gesture

after George Oppen

The question is: How does one hold an apple
Who loves apples

And how does one handle
disaster? The question is

How does one hold a tear
One intends to shed

And how does one endure sadness
If one gives it away.

The Sphere

There it was

bent
axed
pierced
burned
whole parts missing,
a wounded soldier.

Entrance of Battery Park.

It stood there
battered
on a bed of gravel
surrounded by grass.

Signs:

Please do not walk on the grass.
Please do not touch the sphere.

It touched me.

On the gravel:
photos
flowers
gloves
a leather jacket

a picture of the globe as it's been
on the Twin Towers plaza
wrapped in jets of water
blowing mist
of a hot summer day.

Walking # 32

Here there's no fence
no *garde-fou.*
The path skirts the water
so closely you could let the river take you.

Slowly
I step onto the wet grass
separated from myself, as if the side gone
had silenced the other.

Late

It's pouring sadness the color of smoke.
Feel the density of air
the odor of silence across the span of night.

The bodies have turned to souls
then to minds,
yellow irises in the night.

Through a lit window
a shadow moves objects on a wall.
See the flags joining, closing in

the entire map of the world covered with pins
moving, circling as if all that had been,
all that remained had merged into this.

Strange how my life slips away to that house
growing larger past the crowd
beyond that light on the other side of the pain.

On the Podium

The general gave his daily briefings
intimating that our intervention
(it wasn't called "the war" then)
was perfectly tuned and on target;
the troops sufficient, well equipped;
looting normal; torture warranted.
The general stood on the podium—
sly smile, casual wit, paternal,
charming like my father.
(He even looked like my father
telling me how he captured a stag
by the antlers with his bare hands,
all by himself; how the cracks
in the construction he ordered
were planned for expansion.)

I had read in my first primer
the story of the stag subdued by another
as you read in yours that Mary took
her lamb to school and made the children laugh.
But every day (I think it was at noon)
I tuned in to see the general seduce the press
with my father's charm.

A Viewer Like You

After her laundry's been folded,
and her dishes have found their places
on the shelves above the sink,
the old woman sat by herself,
watching young men in army fatigues
fighting in the sand dunes
of a faraway land shooting, shooting,
or being shot dead, or wounded;
and she followed the stretchers
to the ambulances; the coffins
arriving home shrouded in stars;
and she stared at the seven photographs
and the seven names rolling in silence:

Staff Sgt. Nicholas B. Muller,
Sgt. David D. Audo,
SFC. Isaac H. Jackson,
Cpl. Fernando S. Delarosa,
Pfc. Anthony F. Vasquez,
SFC. Mohammed M. Kahn,
SPC. Benjamin D. Manard;

and she recalled the names of fallen
soldiers lining a wall in Washington;
the names on the stones in Arlington;
on the stones in Normandy; and thought
of those not inscribed anywhere.
She remembered the year she spent
at the naval shipyard, drafting plans
of captain's quarters, and machinery,
protected in the centers of ships,
and the enlisted men's berths
unprotected, along the *outer* shells;
and she thought of her grandchildren,
who will one day, some day in their prime,
inherit some war, somewhere…

The Purling River

Fernando Pessoa said:
"The purling river passes and not its sound
which is ours, not the river's."

And I say:
which is the river's as the voice of the deaf theirs,
who only feel its vibration;
as Beethoven's music his, though he couldn't hear it.

"The moon belongs to everyone." And the rivers,
and the seas, and music and science,
and the ugly and the beautiful,

and the lands stretching from one point to another
from one frontier to another,

ours and not.

Sunflowers in August

as Van Gogh never painted them

No yellow, no ochre—fields of dying
suns battered by winds,
an army of soldiers nodding,
feet in the ground, aureoles disheveled,
their crowns blackened by oil; glory
eclipsed by usefulness—

one cup of sunflower seeds
for one half pound sliced almonds
in anything amandine.
The seeds may be whole, slivered
or minced, always *sautéed*
in sunflower oil to bring out their full flavor
in salads, vinaigrettes, entrées or desserts.

Memorial

After my azaleas and rhododendrons
cover themselves with green,
after my tiger lilies wilt, I usually plant
flowering annuals to cheer my summers,
bridging lilacs to chrysanthemums.

Not this year.

This is the year of colored leaves
instead of flowers,
fiery leaves which suddenly appeared
around Manhattan co-ops, where I walk;
along the streets of Brooklyn, where I live;
in Southold, where I sometimes
spend the weekend.

This year,
in this fifth year of the war,
I too planted leaves: incendiary spreads,
yellow-green jagged edged,
red-orange flames, blood-tinted coleus.

Southold

I am on the terrace facing Jockey Creek,
high tide, serene water, fluxed from the bay.
Ed's fishing boat, alongside the restored dock,
awaits the reflux to clear the low bridge.

The sky is pale, chalked with pink light
above the bulkhead cattails,
grass, silvered with dew,
a cluster of dandelions perking up,
though Ed has purged the lawn,
seeded it, and scooped the stubborn weeds.

I love the weeds that flower freely; the scent
of spearmint reborn from old roots; even the geese
trampling over the brand new vegetable patch
and soiling the lawn with smudgy waste.

IV

Ah, the Glitter! (2005)

Ladies and Gentlemen,
buy Woolite.

Dip your sparkling T-shirts
your decorated blue jeans
your Bohemian skirts
in Woolite.

Hang them
and let them dry

'cause rhinestones
beads
glass
sequins
and mirrors
aren't safe for your hands
nor your washer-dryer,

for this summer
as the news gets darker
New York has face-lifted
its stores, its sidewalks
its subway platforms
with the luster
of faraway lands.

Oh the glitter, the roaring twenties!

Homes & Gardens

I

House by the sea

The model as it stood then,
framed in California redwood
on the 9th (?) floor of Macy's Department Store
came completely furnished, landscaped—
waterfront view—for 16 grand.

The living room featured a crackling fireplace
equipped with fake logs and imitation flames.
Above the mantel: a serene painting of the ocean.
The children's room was foam-padded with fairy tales;
the functional kitchen ran on a low electric bill.

The house would be built on Paradise Point
overlooking the Southold Bay (or was it on Promised
Land, facing Cartwright Island?), Gerald and Jacqueline
would share our cost, and we'd alternate weekends,
toasting crabs on the outdoor grill,
gulping raw oysters dashed with lemon.

We would drive past Shelter Island (or
was it Gardiner's Island?), zooming like a speedboat
on the narrow strip with water on both sides.
We'd let the waves lap our toes as our children swam
in the safe harbor. We'd light bonfires on clear evenings
and chant in rounds the songs of our childhood.
Our sons and daughters would collect sunlit
dreams from the moon.
                     16 grand was too much.

II

If you see something, say something
—after Louise Glück

I tell you:
people are burning their own houses.
Every day, new homeless are born,
new luxury condos, new high-rises
in Flatbush, in Sunset Park
where the poor still live.

The poor walk the streets.
They stare into space,
enter stores,
exit stores,
carry groceries.
Their laughter has gone underground.

They wait to be paid to move.
The cost to leave: the price of a house
somewhere else decent,
not in fashion.
Then the sirens tell them
it's time
to pick up their belongings and go.

They will be placed somewhere.
They are eligible
now that they are homeless.

III

The Great Society (1960s)

Before the sun was up, Andon weaved
the new shoots of bindweeds
through the eight-foot link-fence
around our country house
so that the wind made the green
dance around our privacy.
My husband had escaped from Bulgaria
after the war, and believed that private
ought to be private.

Our neighbor, Mr. Fitzgerald,
kept his boxwood enclosure neat
with the help of a shrill hedger.
When its motor paused we thought it
a good time for small talk. Mr. Fitzgerald
kept mostly to himself—door to car,
car to door—when he wasn't attending
his lawn or his hedges.

Sonia was always giving something.
Her property was small,
bordered with hydrangeas.
Here, have some cuttings;
they'll flourish all summer.
Remove the leaves at the base—
that's where the roots will grow.

The Thomases had no enclosure.
They believed in openness.
One lone forsythia decorated their lawn.
One of their daughters worked for the U.S. Mint;

the other, still in college, wore a peace-symbol
T-shirt, and carried a sign at rallies.
The Thomases loved to give advice:
If you have disposable cash, lock certificates in
at 17%. You won't see that again.

With my two children in the rear basket,
I rode a J.C. Penney tricycle—large-front-wheel-
5-speed-easy-to-drive—all over Mastic-Shirley.
I even pedaled the highway to Fire Island
and Southaven Park. I cried when it was stolen.
(The Sears model that replaced it
had small wheels, requiring much effort.)
This is the time when Andon insisted
that we lock our gate night and day;
chain and padlock it.
With so many newly bought houses empty,
you could smell the decay of a philosophy.

On my tricycle
I passed scores of boarded windows
and empty yards where the weeds grew tall,
and I couldn't get a distinctive sense
of the previous owners. Sometimes,
three or four carcasses of dismantled cars
filled the driveways, stripped of everything
worth a penny at the town garage,
but mostly, the houses were bare,
the yards left as bland, as impersonal
as the day they were signed for.

IV

Cafard

You pick these peculiar cockroaches
and give them one by one to the wind—
Carmelian Corbeau versus Joseph Ladouceur
Equitable versus Lydia Grandosa
Affordable versus Susan Bertolini
You versus…You versus…
It's a bad business that drives you-unwilling
corners you into Room 101 Part 18
into Room 409 Room 405 your feet jittering
You versus Time versus Money versus Anger
versus law versus Blackmail versus No More
Sleep…Sleep…on the tree top
Carmelian Corbeau versus Ladouceur
versus you…versus…versus…

V

Open Houses (2005)

We lined them up, by streets, by areas,
by viewing times (11 to 2, 2 to 4, 2:30 to 4)
galloping, breathless, the *Upper West Side*,
the *Upper East*, zooming across in taxi cab or catching
a passing bus not to miss that exquisite jewel at a fraction
of its worth, that bargain-of-a-wreck, my daughter's
fiancé (he's handy) could eventually fix up,
an evening at a time, after a hard day running up
and down industrial complexes, checking, rechecking
that all's properly done, according to contract.

We rushed to visit an "un-renovated
spacious one bedroom with lots of sunlight,
900 sf.; price: $670,000; Maint: $950; 20% down."
The moment we walked in, along with half a dozen
hopeful buyers, we were all scratching
as if we had entered a cavern of microscopic fleas.
The walls were sturdy but the ceiling, crumbling;
and the floor, still impregnated with years of aged
urine, was adorned with newspaper cuttings
over a layer of scent-absorbing bicarbonate of soda.
"This is a good deal," the sales agent said,
"A colleague's showing an identical apartment
on the 5th floor. Renovated. One million two.
Go take a look, and bid if you like."

We left without signing, and later as we sat
recovering from yet another long and fruitless day,
daughter and fiancé decided to hold on to their respective
studios, wed à la Woody Allen / Mia Farrow and wait
for the real estate boom bubble to burst.

Census 2010

I received the census form in mid-March, telling me it only takes a few minutes to answer and send it back. I was waiting for the first of April to fill it in accurately, when on March 24, a postcard arrived advising me that my form wasn't returned yet. How should I know, on March 15 or 24, if I'll still be alive to be counted on the first of April? I am apparently in good health, but who knows—a silent heart failure? I took a plane to and from St. Martin, drove a car. How many car accidents are there every second? (Over six million a year.) And suppose I was living near a volcano, a geologic fault, on the path of a tornado; suppose a terrorist decided to blow up the subway? (I have an unlimited pass and ride it every day, two or three times a day.) On the other hand, my daughter was expecting triplets on April fourth, plus or minus ten days. Another dilemma. Then again, the date—April 1— is April Fools' Day.

The New House

I'm not used to this quiet.
The house exudes Japanese tranquility.
The outdoors comes in
and stays.

After diner, when the children
are sound asleep,
and my daughter and her husband
rest by the fireplace,

I walk through the unlit streets,
avoiding the patches of ice
that have frozen again
after a glorious day of thaw.

I walk. Everyone drives.
The road is forsaken
but for my presence.
I populate it with casual thoughts

of family, of in-laws;
of friendships and intimacies spread
on either side of the ocean
wrapped in ethereal gauze.

I still live at home, in Brooklyn;
only come here once a week, to find out
if at my age I could adjust, adapt and flourish
in a new setting, however beautiful.

V

Crisis

I

Parable of the shrewd steward
—after Luke 16: 1–9

Before leaving his office in disgrace,
the steward invited: friends,
adversaries, the privileged, the neglected
to feast in his employer's wealth.

They all commended the steward
saying he'd done wisely
gracing his way into their future
until . . . it dawned upon them

THEY were his employers.

II

Dear Elaine,

Waking up on November 5th
I thought of your poem "From Lorine:"

Last night
it rained here. Everything
has decided to live.

But then, in a flash:

Cave, sand,
fields of opium
and caravans doing what caravans do.

The route is ours
and we die, we die, we always do.

III

In vain I searched the town

The Lincoln Center grove
that sold ballet outfits for little girls and boys
had closed its doors for good. And in vain
I searched the town for a *Nutcracker* gown
with tiny buttons closing a round collar
and pleats flaring down to the ground
for my little Clara.

Macy's and Conway on Herald Square
carried red plaids, and Bloomingdale's, green;
Disney featured a Cinderella glitzy ball-gown
complete with crown and glass slippers;
Madison Ave. boutiques, skimpy gowns
with beehive stitches, hemmed in red festoons.
Oh where will I find a dainty white gown
with ample pleats flaring down to the ground
for my little Clara?

I may have to sew it myself,
search for a pattern like the ones
from the old Woolworth's, or Singer centers.
The 5 & 10 stores are gone with the wind
and the Singer's I knew, which had moved
from Orchard Street to Borough Hall,
had closed its doors for good.
The only fabric store still standing on the row
sent me cruising to the end of Flatland.
Oh, will I have on time a dainty white gown
with ample pleats flaring down to the ground
for my little Clara?

IV

Preludes
—*after T. S. Eliot*

The winter evening settles down
with images of floods, gusty winds,
blocks of bankrupt retail stores,
and foreclosure signs limning
the deserted streets.

Morning wakes to coffee-stands
attending to the still employed
scurrying to their jobs
and the unemployed searching
for what they had, what's gone.

Why did we think yesterday
that a droplet distilled from dry land,
hurled in disguise across the globe
would form a lasting covenant?

My soul stretches across the sky
that fades behind a city block
at four and five and six o'clock,
unsure that the sun will rise.

V

Everyone forgets that Icarus also flew
　　　　　　　—Jack Gilbert

They were all packing their belongings
into cardboard boxes—
engineering references, precision
instruments, memos: *May 15, 2009—*
This year, the company picnic
will be postponed until further notice.
We hope you'll understand.
That was three months ago.

One forgets past blessings—*Why us?*
We're recession-proof.
The company had been good to them.
Seven years of abundance—now, the fall.

VI

Pies in the Sky

Blueberry pie!
Lemon meringue!
Cherry!
We wanted to give all
a taste of our pies.

We rented trucks (and insured them)
hired drivers (insured them too).
We even insured the pink balloons
tied to each delivery.

It was a jolly time of Blueberry sage,
Paprika marshmallow
Lemon jubilee tied with ribbons
from here to Paris,
from London to Dubai.

So many pies to deliver—
some ended in sewers, some drenched
in floods, whirled in tornadoes.
It rained curried lemon,
blueberries, boysenberries.
Pies dropped from the skies
like deflated balloons;
and the insurance we had popped
like firecrackers on the Fourth of July.

We paid the drivers for the pies they lost;
we paid them for every pie they found,
and paid them again to redeliver them;
we even paid them to retrieve leftover pies.

Oh dire lesson learned if just for an instant:
Now we'll give the sun,
the wind and the magnetic field.

VII

Red-hot Topics

Crude oil slumps
Scientists retool food
Green funerals grow every day.
Sell fast! Sell!

Scientists retool food
Markets surge and tumble
Sell! Sell!
The floor's littered with confetti.

Markets surge and tumble
Crude oil slumps
The floor's littered with bad paper.
Green funerals grow every day.

VIII

A Well-Lit Place

Across the street
from Farrell's
Bar & Grill
where a video store
was unable
to sell old dreams
or revenge
a new pub
just opened its doors.

Drink! Drink!
Let the toasts begin!

A well-lit place,
next to the Wine
& Liquor store
to drown
this sense of dread
this creeping lethargy
as the early evening
steals our pluck.

Drink! Drink!
Let the toasts begin!

IX

The Best of Times

> *Future things are not yet: and if they be not yet,*
> *They are not. And if they are not,*
> *They cannot be seen*
> *Yet foretold they may be*
> *From things present which are already and are seen.*
> —*St. Augustine*

I behold the daybreak, I foreshow
That the sun is about to rise.

Of course Augustine did not have to contend
With the Media, the Dow, the Green,

The pundits *that come and go*
Talking about Robin Hood.

If you don't have a dream
How you gonna have a dream come true?

Nice day, so far, the skeptic says.
The cynic doubts,

And the ideologue objects
For better or worse.

I've seen the summit
Of *this best of all possible worlds,*

I say: *Talk about t'ings you like to do*
And cultivate your garden.

VI

Anti-Novel

Feverish
under the covers

dreaming of a green
summer

I scanned for wit.
(Must've skipped it.)

Rather peculiar
scholarly tidbits

minute autopsies
of minutiae

artfully artless
parodies

Louise Colet's
ramblings

stuffed-parrots
frauds

pink
fading into green

and the eyes (Emma's)
wide open

"black"
under the lashes.

The Year of Magical Thinking

Joan Didion was talking
for at least a half hour when I fell asleep.
She'd been engaged for the hour by Charlie Rose
to discuss her latest book
and I was exhausted by his efforts to draw
out responses worthy of her.

The subject wasn't "her,"
nor her previous works, but grief-talking,
and the enormous task of draw-
ing a life-order through this fall-asleep
wake-up-numb autobiographical book—
a bouquet of memorable quotes, a rose

at a time garnered by Charlie Rose
who seemed quite bored by her
evasion-from-reality mourning
book. Surely, he would prefer talking
politics, or *Salvador*, and not fall asleep
trying to free feeble words, so hard to draw

out. I remember how Didion would draw
characters, from the moment they rose
to the time they fell asleep,
as excerpts from a screenplay, her
protagonists sliced in the middle of talking,
like in the frames for a picture book.

I remember *Play It As It Lays* as a disturbing book.
It, Camus' *Stranger*, Sagan's *Bonjour tristesse* draw
a drifting ennui that affected me. Talking
to her now, I wish host Charlie Rose
would delve into her work, her philosophy, her
influence, so I wouldn't fall asleep

knowing how she fell asleep,
or kept awake, in a reality-avoiding book.
I wonder now if I should read her
Year of Magical Thinking to draw
my own impression, not from Charlie Rose
seemingly bored by her talking.

It may be revealing to follow her trajectory, and draw
reasons for staying asleep after reading an existential book,
or gaining a rose patch from magical talking.

Yesterday Was Saturday

You went to the 9 a.m. Radio City show, fidgeted on a line that turned around the block, gave a dollar, received 10 cents back with your ticket. You sat in the center of a row in the middle of the theater so you won't have to get up for latecomers. You watched the newsreel and two featured films. Did the show come before the films? It's only yesterday and you can't quite remember, but definitely, in one of the films Gregory Peck played a lawyer defending a black man, *To kill—to kill something bird—a Mocking Bird* (and what was the other feature again?), Gregory Peck was superb!

After the show, you went to the drugstore across the street and ordered a chocolate malted milk. The server poured half of it from a tall silver container into a strawed glass you could refill at your ease. The man at your side ordered an *ice cream soda.* (You tried that once and didn't like it.) *Chocolate-malteds* are the best. Also, *Banana-splits* and *Ice cream sundaes.*

*

Yesterday was Saturday. (You were resting after lunch for a two-hour digestion.) Uncle Fernand cupped his hands around his mouth: *Everyone in the water!* You swam two and a half lengths at the bottom of the pool, and shot up. Your head burst, the sky pitch black in the middle of the day, expanding. It's yesterday, and you can't remember what happened next.

*

The man is trying to be pleasant. You think he's courting you. But he's so old—he could be your father. No???? He's eyeing your daughter!

Rain Unending

I could hear the tumult
of each blade of burnt grass,

the despair of frogs
burrowed.

For two months the Earth died
item by item.

until the rain
poured day, and night,

morning, noon, afternoon
as it would never stop

streaming down the rivers
into the sun

down the rivers
the marshes the sea into the sun again,

and the chartreuse, and the green,
and the gold against the blue.

MRI

The technician said it would be long,
to call his name if I want to stop.
His name: Emerson. (How could I forget it?)
Immersed in the tube
my brain scores defects
long neglected, long denied, long accepted—

Blue light—

I'm in Emerson's hands,
his authority on noises-on / noises-off /
blue light / blank / blue / blah…
I've washed my brain of the extraneous
extraneous men pushing buttons.

I'm fastened to a star.

If an object is on a course,
its linear motion won't revert unless
forced, tampered with.
I don't think of growth, not this growth,
when my son has grown happy
and my daughter's many paths converge.

They said one part was at fault,
one soldier the target, one soldier the cause.

The box will tell, the box unwinding the story,
calibrating the dance, unwinding the tune,
deep in the skin, revealing how it severed the moon
on the road to devotion, how it shattered,
how I picked up the pieces one by one.

I'm matter of fact.
I am what I am afraid of.

I'm in my father's hands.
He said I am ancient—and I am,
feel it in my bones,
in the minds of my ancestors collecting
each blown feather back into the pillow.

It's a stalemate,
a complete standstill on the surface
as the figureheads negotiate their assets:
How much does a carrot cost?

How much is a carrot worth?
And how much a blessing?

I am blessed.

Took the seeds and made them grow.

I've done what I could with what I was given,
with what I gave.
I'm blessed.

Blue light. Noise-on-on-on.

Speed is safety. I'm in Emerson's hands.
In the cover of darkness, and in full daylight, flashes—
a crescent of flashes—blue light / blank / blaah.

Black soot.

Eyjafjallajökull

—after Elizabeth Bishop

A volcano has erupted,
the papers say, and last week I was reading
about grounded planes; tourists stranded;
business people far from their destinations,
losing money in the theatres of London,
Paris and Reykjavík.

Well, I had not seen a live volcano before;
only dead ones
with luxuriant rain forest vegetation;
I've seen images of active ones—fearsome,
frightening beauty in motion—
shooting incredible fireworks; spewing
incandescent rivers of lava
obliterating villages in their paths.
But here, all the papers and TV news
have been talking about is: ashes,

ashes, ashes falling down
over Ireland today; Sweden tomorrow;
three thousand kilograms of ashes per second;
one point seven billion's worth of airport
shutdowns and airline delays…
I started losing faith in the *Single
European Sky Project;* I started hating Iceland
and her recurring disasters:
paradise accounts; bank failures;
now a new ash plume is drifting south
bespattering the green fields gray,
poking a hole in the infrastructure.

Do we deserve this? I suppose we must.
What for—I don't know—
not respecting Nature, perhaps.
What did we do to Eyjafjallajökull?
Did we test a nuke under a plateau nearby?

I have a vague recollection of such a thing—
I don't know if it's fact, or dream,
if I've seen it in an action saga
or read it in a book of fiction.
I get confused because I don't know enough.

Why don't I know enough of something?
Geology or skaldic poetry—more regimented
than free verse or free impulse,
a poetry of trochaic or dactylic line endings
that counts syllables as alexandrines do?
I don't like to count, but sometimes,
I do. As an exercise I just tried counting
all the volcanoes on the face of the earth:
the tall, the tiny, the ones that lost
their summits into their magma chambers;
the dead, the dormant, the naughty
and the vengeful that surprise us with terror,
destruction and buried civilizations...

I didn't know that molten lava flows
under the surface of hardened ones; I didn't know
that you can see the molten lava flowing
like a river where the hardened crust has collapsed.
I didn't know that you could witness the sun
rising twice,
once above and once below the clouds
encircling Haleakala.
My sister woke up at four to see it.

I dreamt of my sister last night. Such a joie de vivre!
Despite her pains, she lived fully,
soaking up every moment as if it were her last.
In the dream, she said she was happy.
The surgeon was going to straighten her bones,
give her a new body,
the body she wanted since she was seven.

Moon

There's something powerful
and intimate
in the way the moon pushes and pulls
the waters of the earth; in the way,
in full moon, it breaks the water of mothers;
in the way it befriends a surge of blood
or passion.

I wonder if it does the same
to the air, to the wind.

In hot summer days
I draw in the shady-side air at one end
of my lodging and let it out at the other,
creating a cool breeze I circulate
with the help of fans.

I wonder if the tri-blade farms
that harness the power of the wind
usurp in some way the courtship of the moon.

Sidewalks

In the umber of elm and linden trees
where pedestrians saunter, or stride,
some hundred-year-old bluish slates cave in,
lift corner, or side,
to suit expanding roots.

They let us thump on their raised edges;
let our baby strollers jolt their ups & downs.
They exist to exit—as I do,
as the body does—

until the century-old slates
with their peeled layers,
their ancient unsteady demeanor
are carted away,
and slabs of concrete are poured over gravel.

A Deserving Tree

Rock-a-by baby on the tree top,
when the wind blows, the cradle will rock.
When the bough breaks, the cradle will fall,
and down will come baby, cradle and all.

A lightning rod struck the old oak
shading a park bench across the avenue.
Armed with crane, tape, electric saw,
you only removed its seared crest,

leaving the trunk exposed
to rain, snow storms, hail gusts,
and two heavy limbs, precariously tilting
over babies, sitters, and passersby.

One of the branches fell yesterday
(fortunately during the night)
when babies, sitters, grandparents,
and the concert crowd had gone to sleep.

You hauled away the broken branch,
leaving the other, tilting above the bench.

Summer 2010

It's as if everything were smudged in the background, like in an artist's rubbing, indiscernible and apparently inconsequential. The picture depicts a serene scene—each thing in its place; not a clue left behind: no-knife-no-gun-no-blood-no-poison—(perhaps some slight trace of arsenic; invisible).

In the scheme of things, what's a trace of arsenic? What's a trace of principle that dims or tarnishes an image? The image floats like an idea gone astray; like an obsolete item everyone notices (but no one buys) on the top shelf of a thrift shop.

Perhaps, perhaps next year, if the summer turns temperate; if new water fills the rivers and does not drown the neighborhoods; if the sun eases its rays on our beliefs and endeavors, perhaps, who knows…

What Remains

—after Jack Gilbert

The pine forest, the mountains and their crevices,
the red earth faded. They were the background,
not the soul. The little Church of the Visitation
with its bright stained-glass Elizabeth
welcoming Mary vanished with my faith.

Aunt Marguerite is indelible.
She read to us, all of us in nightgowns,
sitting cross-legged on her bed—
Les Malheurs de Sophie and all the Comtesse de Ségur,
and all Jules Verne disappeared with childhood.
Rostand emerged with panache.

Simone Jourdan, a close friend, died.
Joelle Parmentier got fat and distant.
I fell in love, in love as all that existed was him.
And I was nothing at all. And I had to move away
not to see him, never to see him again.

The Hudson River was a comfort—
furrows of passing barges; ripples on the gravel;
shimmer of calm reflection—
my new life burgeoned over the old. But sometimes,
when I do something I shouldn't have, I hear myself say:
Max me prend dans ses bras et me dit qu'il m'aime.
If I catch the mantra in time, I cut it short.
My first love, he, I could've died for: an exorcism,
a mere mantra with no emotion, no attachment.

City College lasted. The diction class did not
—the teacher saying: *No, Nicole. Like in French;*
and I, saying *Chandelier* as in French;
and the teacher again: *No-no-no. Shan-de-leer—*
the diction with the enormous effort never took root.
Grammar, syntax, perfect and pluperfect
lasted through the years.

Father died. Then, Mother. They are still with us.
Andon's phantom still whispers, and sometimes shouts.
My little sister Monique expired in a puff
like a burning flame—put to rest.
She lives with the rest of us, miles apart.

Morning with Pessoa

—Cento from his uncollected poems

This morning I went out very early,
Because I woke up even earlier
And had nothing I wanted to do.

There is in each thing an animating essence.
In plants it's a tiny nymph that exists on the outside.
In man it's the soul that lives with him and is him.
And I, who have eyes that are only for seeing,
See an absence in all things.

The child knows how it is that things exist.
He knows existence exists and cannot be explained,
And he knows that to exist is to occupy a point.
What he doesn't know is that thought is not a point.

Today I wish I could think of Spring as a person.
But Spring isn't even a thing:
Nothing returns, nothing repeats.
Not even the flowers or green leaves return.
There are new flowers, new green leaves.
For me this sun,
These meadows, these flowers are enough.
But if they weren't enough,
What I would want is a sun more sun than the sun,
Meadows more meadows than these meadows,
Flowers more flowers than these flowers—
Everything more than what it is in the same way,
The same manner.

I lifted my right hand to wave at the sun,
I was glad I could still see it.

102

Notes

Page 25—"The eyes we close": Cento made of lines by John Ashbery, Elaine Equi, Sully Prudhomme and Paul Verlaine.

Page 40—*Cervelle en Beignets:* Fried Brains

Page 68—*Cafard:* Cockroach; *Fam.:* Dark thoughts

Page 76—In the poem "Dear Elaine," the quote is from Elaine Equi's book, *Voice Over.*

Page 83—"The best of Times" lines in Italics from St. Augustine, T. S. Eliot, Oscar Hammerstein, Stephen Dunn, and Voltaire.

Page 87—"Anti-Novel" refers to *Flaubert's Parrot* by Julian Barnes.

Page 98—"Morning with Pessoa" Cento excerpted from *Fernando Pessoa & Co* uncollected poems, edited and translated from the Portuguese by Richard Zenith.

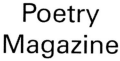

WITHDRAWN

CPSIA information can be obtained at www.ICGtesting.com
Printed in the USA
BVOW011406131212

308154BV00002B/98/P